wild places

S U P E R I O R'S
NORTH SHORE
wild places

PHOTOGRAPHY by jay steinke

To Dave & Sue,
with much appreciation
for your encouragement
over the years!

tea table books
DULUTH, MINNESOTA

Right photo - Mood altering storm clouds
push the scent of snow over
the sparkling waters of the
Great Lake.

First Frontispiece - Ice Shards, Grand Marais
Second Frontispiece - Spring Break Up,
Beaver River

Publisher: Tea Table Books
1831 East Third Street
Duluth, MN 55812

Printer: Walsworth Printing
Marceline, MO.

Book Design: Sandra Ettestad

Copyright © Jay Steinke 1993

ISBN: 0-9635871-0-2

The birthplace of this book is far from Superior's North Shore. I was raised near another Great Lake . . . Michigan. My childhood memories are filled with many adventures of exploration along its shores. My love for the Great Lakes has continued into my adult life but now my attention centers on Lake Superior.

My purpose for producing this book is to share my affection for the North Shore with both residents and visitors. During the last 10 years, the footprints of civilization have become more evident along the shore, and I felt a strong desire to show the path to wild places is still wide open.

The North Shore of Lake Superior has one of America's most magnificent shorelines. I have spent countless hours affirming this fact by exploring, and photographing, its shores, rivers and forests. The images contained in this book offer my personal vision and reflections of this scenic region. Inside you'll experience my visual response to the moods and personality of the North Shore. With each photograph, I strive to identify and depict the emotion of the moment. Every composition carries with it a life, a memory and a story of its own. It is my desire that these images will create in you a greater appreciation for the "Wild Places of the North Shore."

jay steinke

Once a detour on the voyageur's highway,
Pigeon Falls still thunders with warnings of power.

The personality of time is etched in the face
of tattered bluffs that make up Split Rock State Park.

Cedar sentries stand a wet watch
over the lower falls in Gooseberry State Park.

The personal fortunes I seek on my photographic explorations into wild places are jewels that enrich the soul and the body. The gems that best describe my work are peace and quietude. During my travels, I keep my eyes open wide in search of images that best convey these qualities in nature.

An area where my treasure hunts have been especially rewarding lies near the Canadian border in the hills around Mt. Josephine. From the vantage point where this photograph was taken, I have heard the mating call of bull moose echo up from the valleys. I have seen bald eagles patrol their majestic domain of wilderness. I have imagined voyageurs hiking these hills in quest of their own fortunes. On this day, I discovered a bounty of tranquillity as silver shadows of fog ebbed and flowed over the land like a slow motion, air-borne wave.

Wild Roses gathered in a birch corral
sweeten the air of a North Shore summer day.

Echoes of green on the still waters
of Bean Lake reflect the promise of spring.

One of the things I like best about the North Shore is the door of discovery is always wide open. The day this photograph was taken, I was experiencing a curious mood of exploration. I felt the need to gaze at a view I'd never seen before. I wasn't sure if it was a river canyon, a flower filled meadow or a backlit forest silhouette. But I knew I'd recognize it once I saw it.

As I followed a small river valley northward, I entered one of the most striking birch forests I have ever seen. 🍃 Thousands of stately white birch standing tall in a sea of lush green leaves and underbrush. Halfway through the birch woodland I heard the sound of water rushing. But it wasn't the usual river roar, it was more like sheets of rain slicing through air.

I moved forward and finally located the source of this peculiar North Shore song. It came from a stretch of river where ribbons of white water were sliding over shelves of time-polished rock. I took this photograph and then settled back to let its melody work its way into my soul.

Yellow Lady's Slippers dance toward the sun
in a green ballroom of balsam boughs.

A crisp North Shore afternoon beams
a kalidescope of color from Carlton Peak.

Highway 61 is the black ribbon that rolls along the North Shore from Duluth into Canada. As soon as you head north out of the Twin Ports, a tug-of-war for your attention begins in earnest. On your right, the ongoing visual impact of Lake Superior calls out . . . to your left, the rivers, forests and high country of the shore pull your eyes inland.

For me, the longer the ride north, the better I like it. Perhaps that's why many of my favorite North Shore destinations are between Little Marais and Pigeon River. One location I keep returning to, especially when there's a soft fog, is the Temperance River.

The Temperance is an active river in a hurry to offer its contribution to Lake Superior. But despite its turbulent nature, the Temperance always offers a number of reflective vantage points where you can watch its waters race southward through an obstacle course of twists, turns, funnels and cascades. This photograph was taken right after a brief rest stop along its rocky bank. I had repacked my gear then continued my hike down river. Just before I rounded a bend, I turned and discovered this scene. It's one spot, among many, where the river and surrounding wilderness proudly display their personality.

Oberg Mountain watches the morning light
dissolve the final remains of a rain soaked night.

The jagged peaks of the Sawtooth Mountains
frame a Lake Superior evening from Artist's Point
in Grand Marais.

I believe anyone who visits the Witch Tree will experience its influence in one form or another. The enchantment begins as you hike to the tree through one of the only moss enshrouded forests on the North Shore. After a soft, quiet walk you reach the tree and soon realize . . . this is an extraordinary place.

My visits here always generate in me emotions of reflection and reverence. On the day of this photograph, I caught glimpses of 300 years of history this Spirit Tree has witnessed. From its rocky perch above the lake, the tree has received generations of Ojibwa and watched the canoes of French voyageurs and explorers pass before it. The Witch Tree also speaks of life, growth, hardship, strength and character. One day it will speak about death . . . but not yet.

Today it continues its watch over the North Shore. It still weathers Superior's destructive November gales that can break steel ships but not the Witch Tree. Although bent and twisted, it still stands straight and tall as a living symbol of wild places.

*Spring rains carve their way through a series
of waterfalls on the Cascade River.*

After spending the night in a winter campsite, I rolled out of my sleeping bag into the black morning of a 15 degree day and made my way through snow and dark to the spot I had selected for this shot.

I framed my camera on the desired composition, then shivering, settled back to wait for the first faint fingers of dawn to touch me. Peering through the darkness, I became aware of another message my senses were sending me . . . silence. 🌙 There wasn't a whisper of wind, only the gentle sound of water lapping at a thin layer of newly formed ice.

Within a short time, the horizon began to widen with the spreading color of reds, pinks and purples. This time I shivered with the privileged pleasure of being able to witness this new beginning. When the reflections and light were right, I made my exposure and then lingered to catch the encore of the sun cresting over the dividing line of lake and sky. All in all, a memorable way to start a new day in a wild place.

Near Grand Marais, a crescent moon winks
its approval of the colorful approach of a new day.

An early moon set over the Suzie Islands
bids good morning to Long Island flowers.

A lthough each North Shore season brings its own unique package of visual gifts, fall seems to make the boldest bid for my attention. In answer to its colorful call, I made an appointment with the setting sun and started out in the late afternoon for Leveaux Mountain with my dog Casey.

We waded through a sea of golden maple leaves, crossed the Onion River, hiked along the base of ascending bluffs, and traversed the switchbacks that led to the peak. I had made the same journey the day before to scout shooting locations and discovered this weathered pine. But to capture this image, I had to climb out on a narrow rock point. A high wind prevented this shot so I made plans for the return visit.

I wasn't disappointed. The twilight calm seemed to hold those fleeting moments when the setting sun fired the forest canopy with a golden glaze. I made my exposure wishing I could stop time to savor the view. In moments like these, it's hard not to let your heart beat out an appreciative applause for nature's curtain call.

Autumn leaves mingle with the Onion River
and together they join in the journey to Lake Superior.

The sky, land and lake surrounding Stony Point
display the visual benefits of a sub-zero day.

A long the North Shore, winter can be a quick change artist that lays down a thick blanket of snow, cold and ice one day and then throws back the covers the next day to reveal a clear, serene world. The day after one of our famous Minnesota blizzards, I wanted to take advantage of the fresh snow and blue skies so I grabbed my snowshoes and decided to scout the area around Raven Lake.

As I topped a small rise, the scene in this photograph caused me to pause. I was about to continue forward, but something held me in check. It was the undisturbed beauty of this place. 🐾 Not wanting to leave my mark on this newly laid carpet of white, I edged along the perimeter of the knoll to locate the best composition for the image.

I took this shot, then detoured around the birch hill so this setting would always remain in my mind just the way I found it . . . undisturbed.

The frosty brush of winter transforms a canvas of evergreen into a wonderland of white.

*Fireweed surrounding Good Harbor Bay brings color
to the fog shrouded waters of Lake Superior.*

A lone spruce bows to the power and majesty
of Lake Superior on a quiet, foggy day near Two Harbors.

As a landscape photographer, I bring my own unique perspective to the way I view our world. A statement I once read helps me interpret my personal expressions of this art form. It said, "Nature is the art of God." It's a sentiment I embrace as I approach nature through my viewfinder and attempt to capture on film the messages creation speaks to me.

This perspective was in full operation during a recent drive to Grand Portage. I was glancing at Lake Superior when my eye caught the brilliant white flowers of this serviceberry tree. I stopped, approached the tree and began to study it for composition. Everything fit . . . fragile white blossoms bathed in warm sunshine, an infinite blue backdrop, a definition line of water-worn rock and the youthful face of Superior without wrinkle or blemish. I took this photograph and today it still serves as a peaceful reminder that nature offers a personal message for anyone who has eyes to see and ears to hear.

Lichen covered rock fingers reach
into the cool pockets of a Lake Superior morning.

Once the light of life for mariners,
Split Rock Lighthouse is still a beacon
for North Shore visitors.

I n landscape photography, there are certain shots that demand certain conditions. On an earlier trip I had discovered this vantage point near Belmore Bay and vowed to return when the next nor'easter began to blow. On this day, the weather cooperated beautifully for the image I wanted to capture. Wind gusts up to 30 MPH were driving waves, rain and drizzle across Lake Superior and slamming all three into the North Shore.

Fortunately the wind was at my back, and the camera was sheltered as I waited for the perfect wave. But one wave looks a lot like the last one, so I shot exposure after exposure and became colder, wetter and colder still. Then it happened. A huge swell moved in. With the last exposure on the roll, I clicked the wave just at the precise moment it broke over the point and sent its angry plume into the gray sky.

After this shot, as I stood on those thundering shores, I realized I was a ringside witness to the explosive power of nature. Superior had again defended its title as the world's greatest lake.

For information on ordering,
Jay Steinke's original,
signed photographs:

Jay Steinke Photography
1831 East Third Street
Duluth, MN 55812
Telephone: (218) 728-6046

Acknowledgments

Sandra Ettestad, my heartfelt thanks for all you have
given to this book, from designing and producing it
to your encouragement which was a strong force in
bringing it through the dream stage.

Glen Carlson, thank you for being a part of this book
by taking my thoughts, feelings and experiences and
putting them into words. They have added a new
dimension to the photography.

To the many people up and down the shore who
granted me permission to explore on their property.